CW00858826

Tartan and Turmeric

Leela Soma

ISBN-13: 978-1987612424

ISBN-10: 1987612426

Also by the author

Poetry

From Madras to Milngavie

Novels
Twice Born
Bombay Baby

Short Stories
Boxed In

For my family

Contents

Gayatri Mantra

Asato mā sad gamaya

Tamaso mā jyotir gamaya

Mṛtyormā amṛtam gamaya

Aum śānti śānti śāntiḥ (Upanishad 5000 BC)

From ignorance, lead me to truth;
From darkness, lead me to light;
From death, lead me to immortality
Om peace, peace, peace

‘

He is never born, and never dies.
He is in Eternity…
He does not die when the body dies'
The Bhagavad-Gita Gita (c.500 BC)

Light

A road, an unknown path, a familiar quest
In the inroads of our being, not in rest
Still night, words unspoken, sobs, mark
Flesh, bone, cremated ashes, from dust to dust.
Reincarnating life anew, *Maya* releases the shadow
All that remains is a gossamer reflection of yesterday's lives.

In darkest sorrow we desire, the impression of life
A mother, father, a child, a soul remembers
By material things are memories made
A sari, a thumbed book, an unopened satchel
A life unfulfilled in our mind's eye.

While bright Consciousness, the Light Eternal
Moves on to the ether world
We mourn.
Life continues.
Glossary- (Maya- Unreal/Illusion)

Published in Gutter Magazine Issue (05)

Slumdog

Yes I am a slum dog, an orphan, an urchin of the street
My world revolves around the next meal, a day since my last
My little brother is eight, yes, that lame boy, I am all he has
I run over to your car, I rap on the clean window for a few *paisa*

The driver shoos me, throws me a dirty glance and shakes his fist
Your brow is knitted; you wipe the tiny dots of sweat with silk
You look away. Is the air-conditioner in the car not working?
Are you sweltering in the warmth of a guilt-ridden heart?

The light changes, your revved car shoots forward, I slump back
I run to the pavement and join my brother crouching under the shade
Of the straggly old tree, brown and dying slowly in the heat and dust
He looks up, his parched, dry lips salty white at the edges.

I remember my mother's crumbling body, as near starvation slowly took its toll
Her pleading eyes and words, 'always look after *'langda'*, he needs you
Her strength, her love, her hard work till her dying day gives me the mettle to
Survive; I live on the streets, a *chai* here and a bite there and hold onto my brother

The only precious thing, she left behind.

Glossary:
Paisa: pennies
Langda: Lame person
Chai – Tea

The Missing Anklet

No trial, truth murdered in cold blood, an innocent man slain.
 Kannagi stormed the palace in rage, the woman's wrath unrestrained
At the palace the diamonds spilled forth from the anklet she threw on the floor
Her anger glinted in flawless brilliance, reflected bright on mirrored door
The pearls on the queen's ankle quivered, the rubies contained.

The court rose as one, the voice loud across the brocaded expanse
'I demand justice,' the cry of the brave widow rent the air, her trembling stance
As she held her other anklet high and cursed *Madurai* be raised by fire
Enflamed, the truth emerges, king relents, and history records her ire.

'Silapathikaram' (5th C BCE a Tamil epic.)

Glossary:

Kannagi-Legendary Tamil woman is the central character
in Silapathikaram a South Indian Epic. She took revenge on
the king of Madurai, for a mistaken death penalty imposed on her
husband by cursing the city to be burnt down.

Madurai: A city in South India

Published in 'The Bangalore Review'

Diwali

Diwali the festival of lights

That ends evil after a protracted fight
when good with all its might
leads us from darkness to Light.

When old and young with delight meet
with love and affection all hearts beat.

That gracious festival which celebrates victory
keeps alive the ancient festival of myth and mystery.

Sari

Six yards of silk or cotton draped around the waist

Saffron hues, peacock blue, iridescent flame of the forest

Gold and silver embellished borders on the fabric

Designs handed down over generations ago

Painted on canvas, hewn in sculptures of bronze and stone

A sari encapsulates the Indian culture.

Village River

The river winds its way, meandering round the village
Pale blue or green, changing colours like a chameleon
Fresh to bathe, wash clothes and fill the day's needs in the pots
Women carry the precious resource on their heads, while
Children splash about in the heat of the day cooling their bodies.
Water, food, a roof over their heads and clothes, simple things
That their mothers scrape together to fulfil their basic needs.

As shining India races forward, the West vying
For a place in the new emerging country of wealth
Invests in sweatshops, eyes the market, wants a slice of the cake,
Allures the middle class consumers, ignores the poor as they huddle
In huts that crumble under the bulldozer, a slum cleared again
For a new shopping mall aglow with designer ware, enriches
A corrupt politician as he pockets the bribes, his future assured.

A nuclear dawn, for an ancient country with a rich heritage
Indulges with satellites in the skies, more weapons to show that
on the world stage, might is right, plays the game, stakes are high.
While the old river in the village meanders calmly, brown with
sludge of the factories that blight its banks, infect the people
no longer the fresh water to rely on, the thirst of the poor
quenched by sugary drinks and empty promises, as mothers struggle.

Resolve

A child bride married at ten, a mother at thirteen
The fate of many grandmothers in the last century
Children betrothed at birth, promised to each other
To unite families to keep farms and lands intact

She had to blend into an extended family, the norm
A life of service to one and all, childhood sacrificed
Her young body and mind steeled in resolve, strong
 To flow with the tide, her choice was not an option.

No birth control, no voice for this child bride
She carried on quietly bearing with fortitude
The vicissitudes of what life threw at her
She laughed and cried when the sun smiled.

(Published In the Poetry Shed, 2015)

New Year

Vishu, the New Year begins in the soft early dawn
A bleary eyed wakening to the exciting day of sweets
 New silken clothes rustling, Pujas and feasts on banana leaves
Mother wakes her to open her eyes, guides her to the decorated altar
Morning dazzled by the offerings of fruit, honey, sweets
To Lord Krishna, the lover of butter and maidens fair
She's entranced by the picture of him playing the flute
And her childish heart hopes the New Year is full of fun.

Note: Vishu is the name for New Year celebrations in Kerala.
"Yesterday is but a dream,
*Tomorrow is only a vision"- **Kalidasa***

Mother Earth

Mata Bhumih putro ham prithvyah

(Earth is our mother and we are its children.)

Mother Earth, the woman I first knew
Existence borne on your brown matter

Glorified, reviled as mother, goddess or wife
Giving birth shaping all beings good and bad

A virgin a wife, a snake to beguile the first man
Fruit, sweet and tempting to gather sin

Often sinned against holding up half the sky or
Bending to scratch a living to feed another mouth

Raped, sold, circumcised, exploited in war and peace
Honored, revered when needed, the recipient of seed

Life would be nonexistent, woman is the giver of
Breath, birth, care and nourishment to mankind.

Earth mother is treated likewise, a pale reflection
Of woman on earth, abused and neglected.
Published in *'Steel Bellow'* magazine Buffalo USA (2016)

Chaturanga

Chess using dice, an ancient Indian invention
Throwing a piece of rock or bone marked for a game,
 Chaturanga, or chess, played by kings and queens of yore.
Four divisions of the military, cavalry, infantry, elephants and
chariotry
Transformed into the rook, knight, bishop and king
A game of strategy that harks back to an eastern civilisation,
Played today by millions around the world.

Tartan & Turmeric

Six yards of wool wound around the waist
Colours of thistle purple, rowan red, laced
With deep blue of the sky-reflected sea
And bright emerald of verdant grass, dyes
Criss-crossed in tartan so unique, the kilt
That chequered history of Scottish culture.

A yellow humble herb growing wild
The turmeric with antiseptic qualities
Unearthed by ancient Indian wisdom
Growing popular like Yoga, worldwide
Part of my heritage that colours me
Both supplanted in the West.

Tartan and turmeric a strange duo
Five thousand miles of separation
Joined together in this globalised world
Oneness, unity in diversity, cultures shared,
Tea and cotton, jute and jam, silk and wool,
They are the warp and weft of my being.

(Published in *Steel Bellow* magazine Buffalo USA 2016)

The Kibble Palace

Glasgow's Botanics, a green scene with flowers bright in summer

Lush and pretty all year round, an oasis was The Kibble Palace

A Victorian concept cherished and restored in the West End

In my homesick mind I made the glass structure my own.

Inside, the banana tree with its broad fronds stood erect.

The tiny fruits in bunches, hung together, a dark green, in tight clusters.

The warmth was a welcome respite from the cold, damp and grey outside.

Transported to my sub-tropical home, I savoured, nay, devoured the surroundings.

A home from home, my skin warmed in that heat, the familiar plants of areca,

And turmeric, whole palm trees huddled in the bright space

Well cared for, nurtured and protected from the harsh winter outside

Transported me to the brown mother earth of India.

'Vasudaiva Kutumbakam' -The whole earth is a family

Published in Glasgow West End: Pat's Guide

Gaun's Pool

In gentle Morayshire the Gaun's pool swirls below the bridge
The test bed of ancient witches still casts its strange aura
Flung into the pool from the Gaun's stone they had no escape
If they sank they were innocent, if they floated, the poor
women
Deemed to be guilty, were dragged out and put to death.
Women condemned as witches in a man's world.

Note: Keith in Moray where this took place.

Pearl

In South Island seas, Brander's fortune was founded
Trading coconuts by the million, and black pearls
Filled the ships that sailed the mighty seas, he sent
Exotic goods so favoured by Europe from the Pacific
Pearl-shell for the swanky houses of Paris he gave
The pearl culture enhanced the treasures of the rich.

Tetuanui i reia i te Raiatea, her very name a song
The fourteen year old Tahitian Princess stole his heart,
Cut off from the aquamarine waters of her birth.
A woman of substance she bore him nine children,
An esteemed socialite, her parties were legion
The first lady of Tahiti did Scotland proud.

On Brander's death Anstruther gained the princess
In a tiny fishing village in Fife, she flourished
Married again she mothered three more children.
She lies buried in the parish churchyard faraway
From the turquoise lagoons, a paradise on earth
That Gauguin chose to paint in vibrant colours.

Note: The Princess died in 1898 and her gravestone
Can be seen in Anstruther Parish church.

(Published in STANZA-Poetry Map of Scotland)

Strawberries

Luscious,

Delicious, Scrumptious,

Creamily,   Slobbery,

Dribbly,

Yummily

Jammily,   Fruity,

Spanish   Scottish

On scones or trifles

Lush.

Three posies

The earthquake shattered the tiny island
Tsunami flooded the cracked earth
People in their thousands dead or lost
Babies cuddled by shocked parents in vast tents
Motorways rent asunder towns in disarray
Scenes unimaginable challenges not to look away
Rooted and shaken as we try to help

The bemused tenacity of the child orphan
The humbling grief of an older widower
The lame woman hobbling to help others
The infinite patience of the rescue teams
The images seared in us forever
Moving, touching our lives faraway
News moves on to the next disaster

Of all the touching scenes of devastation
One image stands out so clearly
The quiet dignity of a proud race
The kindness of a sensitive soul who
Provided baths, showers in a tented space
Warm clean water to cleanse fear and
Three posies placed in tiny vases on a table.

(A tribute to Fukushima nuclear disaster)

The Proposal

Bright candle sheds a soft glow
Shadows on the wall act a play
The young couple's eyes glistening
Each drinking the smile in the other

The blue tip haloes around the orange flame
Searing, melting, liquefying hot, her blush spreads
The tiny wick spurred on by the dripping wax waits still
He leans over opens a box and a diamond dazzles

Her eyes widen her happiness etched deep as he kneels
The candle flame's golden flecks in her eyes brighten
They seal their union with a kiss, and
The flames dance on the wall.

Black and White

The cinema drowned in darkness creepy scene of rows of seats

Black and white scenes roared on screen, Pathe news in clipped tones

Fear gripped throat tightened as the main horror film music played

A score that stayed in the head to scare one at night safely tucked in bed.

Values

Places of worship bring forth the best in man
Art and literature reaches unknown heights
Spiritual music feeds the soul and touches the heart
Architecture that amazes the eyes and the senses

Yet the temples, mosques, churches and chapels
Destroyed by man, making and unmaking history
Stirring deep passion, loyalties inured over centuries
Fought over time, generations shedding their blood.

Thoughts that affect the psyche nurtured from the crib, as
The world fights for justice against fundamentalism
A law to change hearts and minds that remain unmoved
Hard, unchanging in the deep brush strokes of hate.

Future

Hope is the child of the unborn future
Life's lessons may strain and stress
The lay of the land not always at its best
Floods, earthquakes and terror strikes fear
Yet hope strides and refreshes
The one overriding truth
The future is carved out in the present.

Goodbye

A life time together happy and content
Cameos together in the framed picture
Memories re-lived in the old tunes
Broken handles pots and pans familiar
One's life marked on so many surfaces
Canvas, paper, fabric scented with her life.

 Now charity bags filled with possessions
Drawers emptied a sob-wrecked separation.

Grief encompasses the sheltered home
Hovering relatives and whispering hordes
Tea and sympathy that can't undo
A cancerous death so cruel

Yet uplifted by the glance of
The baby granddaughter's toothless smile
Crawling helplessly, hugging her so close
The curl of her lips and shape of her eyes
Imprinted on the child, helps remind of the family line.

(Published in Rat's Ass Review)

Gallery

The artist's palette with colours of every hue
The brush strokes on canvas a picture make
Framed and hung high in a silent gallery with care
Each room evoking, pulsing with emotions bare

Oils bases recreate a scene
Tugs the heart, a cord struck clean
Almost taste the bite of a still life fruit
Hear the dress rustles of a lady fair
Or the touch of cold marble sculpture rare

Senses rise to the fore, centuries of skill withstood
The test of time and more
Nature bestowed landscapes to sketch fine
The canvas makes me hold this breath of mine.

Rainbow

Disappears in a thin shower of rain
The seven colours of the rainbow
Iridescent and bright, a bow of eternal beauty
Indigo rich and burnt orange
Yellow smooth and red vibrant
Streaks the blue sky and reflect
On the lush green below and
Colours the earth, gives us its brilliant shades.

Camera

The camera of the mind burnished with images past
Of family groups and friends entwined or lost
Sepia images browned edges and memories bitten and chewed
Brought to colour at weddings festivals to be renewed

Photo albums stacked in a box out of fashion, aged and frayed
Sepia a shade of old, of tales never told of some who had strayed
Vellum bound on blank pages stuck in a time warp of its own.

Images now in colour bright and bold
Clicked and digitalised in a moment's hold
Face Booked, Twittered and shown to the world
Cameras shy an unfamiliar word, unwritten and cold.

Quest

After it rained the aroma sand-toasted
Filled in as the night drew humid hot roasted
Tropical dark a new moon sky splattered
Tiny star –gemmed the points begging to be smothered
The scent of jasmine night queen waft
Darts of chameleon on the areca nut bark
Croaking cicadas unfettered night song
Sleepy willows hang down in languid limbs
A road a path unknown a familiar quest
In the inroads of my being not rest
Who am I? Why am I here?
The universe has the answers
Not I.

Water boarding

The pool looked serene, the blue of the chlorinated water soft to the
eye
Scanning the scene the young ones splashing about with inflatable
balls
A gentle swim with the head above the water, breaststrokes, few
lengths
Relaxed and cool, the sun dappling on the trees outside streaking
new colours

A dare to try the new flumes, looked like fun, easy as a flowing river
Downstream all the way with no effort at all, no challenge at all
Should one try something that augurs a fear that cannot be
explained?
A walk up the steps queuing with the youngsters, colour rising
cheeks.

Festival lights

The season to light the fire and bring forth joy in the parlour
In the winter month lamps and tea lights are ablaze lending colour
As light sheds its glow and dispels the dark
Sparklers fizz, fireworks blaze a trail in the sky and rids the murk
The raging storm and freezing sleet are kept at by
As we *coorie* in snug in the warmth of a festival day
For a lamp in a windless place does not flicker.

A smile

Selfishness taught by the intrusive media
The need to become a celebrity in this soulless world
Community is an unfamiliar world, in this unethical place
Survival no longer is subsistence, more a collection of material
things
Wants becomes needs, the adverts convinces us that 'I am worth it'

Mores, norms shifted away, the rude rules the world
The generation follows 'advanced' in science and materialism
Simple things have lost their meaning, a scrabble for them by
The older people given short shrift, the planet earth moves on
Civilisation has forgotten the simple things in life
Kindness? Who needs it in this age of plenty?

Old lessons learnt over millions of years is stowed away
A smile you sent will always return never resurfaces
Until mother nature enforces on the subconscious the horror of
A tsunami or earthquake shuddering the people back out of
Complacency and new fears fill the void of that deep fear.

Spring

Blue skies, sun streaming, spring leaves burnished gold
The flowers in bud catching the warmth to softly open
Their perfumed beginnings to enchant, entice the bees
Life all around starts its circle, a small beginning
Born again, reincarnated, new avatars rejuvenated
Spring has sprung, its glory etched on eggs
Rolled down hills, wild with frail little daisies.

Vermillion

Leaves fall down, blown away in the autumnal blitz
Gold strewn paths crunch and crackle underfoot
A single vermillion leaf like a tear drop stands proud
Defiant, blood red, life courses through its veins.
The widow looks askance; the blood red leaf sends a shiver
An awakening of the day as her *sindoor* on her forehead is
wiped away
The *bindu*, the dot, the point at which creation begins, negated
forever
The jangle of broken glass as bangles are crushed, ornaments
discarded
The white sari envelopes her shroud-like, a colourless palette
A life of the walking dead bereft of feelings, love or emotion.
Vermillion turned to ash, grey, unassuming as the leaden
skies.
The blood red leaf trodden under the walker's brisk steps
A lifeless mess of veins traces its lineage etched on the path
Submerged, in the brown heap of dead leaves.

Published in 'I am a Silent Poet'

Koorma Avatar

Like the *Koorma* avatar, a strong tortoise shell to bear the
weight of
The *Mandar* mountain, face the vicissitudes that life hands
you,
Delve deep into your soul to find passion, love and care.
Search for
The nectar of life, the fourteen precious skills to forge forward
Find the immortality of peace; churn the ocean of milk of
human kindness
Discover it lying dormant, that is deep within you, then prise
it open
With acts of *seva*, to fulfil your spirit and spread joy to all.

Emotions that churn inside, one's life is never bereft
Of waves of joy and deep sorrows, a veritable ocean
That sways one's being. If thoughts dwell on the negative,
It rocks the soul to bitterness. But breakaway, like the
White foam that merges into the sand and sea, reinvent each
day,
Flow back on the crest of a new wave and delight in the
warmth
Of the sun of a new day, fresh as the dew tipped dawn.

Published in Visual Verse

Ardhanarishvara

Androgynous, half male half female, split down the middle
Synthesis of the *Purusha* and *Prakriti* male, female energies
Its union the root of all creation, where opposites merge
Inseparable as word and its meaning, instilled in our
consciousness.

Or is it the progress of civilisation that subtly transforms
That synergy to inequality, the might over right
Cartoonised in shades of purple and blue
The female reduced imperceptibly
Smaller, weaker
Marginalised?

Published in Visual Verse

Avvaiyar

Avvaiyar, music bears her verses, lyrics dripping like honey
From the heart of this woman of yore, a god given talent
Cherished by the Tamil kings of the *Sangam* period
Songs of Universal truths, that evoke the past, present and
future.

The oral tradition lives on, learnt by rote, passed down
unhindered
By the centuries and tidal waves of alien cultures, her
beautiful words
Etched in the soul of Tamils, a culture, preserved later in the
volumes of
The *Athichuvadu,* written on palm leaves, before the advent of
papyrus.

Her fifty nine verses of pure gold, in scriptures of old
The *Purananuru,* four hundred poems in the *Akaval* meter,
Relished and imparted to this day. It rolls off the tongues of
The young and the old, a legacy, belonging to an ancient
culture,
Untouched by time, is ageless, traced and crystallised in her
verses.

Sangam Period: From 3rdC BC to 4th C AD
Athichuvadu, Purananuru are titles of her famous works.
Her words: *"What you have learned is a mere handful; what you
haven't learned is the size of the world"* are exhibited *at NASA*
*(http://www.nasa.gov/audience/foreducators/informal/features/F_Co
smic_Questions_prt.htm)*

I am Me

You told me mother
Loud and clear
Work harder
Be twice as good
We need to do better
To get anywhere

Never forget your roots
Your proud heritage
Your language, your culture
Take the best of both
Blend it well
Make it your own
Here I am mother

A barrister to prove by
Working hard
Being nicer and
Done all I can
I have reached my goal
Never perfect I try

Blending the best that
I can find in me
Neither an Indian in India
Nor a Scot in Scotland
I am me

'The mud is the truth in all the pots'- Bhagavad-Gita

Origins

The alien culture may subsume the inborn
The veneer accepted to survive, find our way
In a strange land, chosen for comfort,
Wants steeps over the innermost needs,
 We try hard to assimilate.

The roots put down, life pleases in ways imagined
Luxury to behold, happiness brushes the surface
The newness enthrals, we accumulate more, the
Pleasure never wanes; life is exulting as we race
Up the ladder of achievement, showcased to the world.

Now, as the next generation buds into reality, values
of old reappear, the cadence of the mother-tongue,
suckled with love at birth, skin on skin, the taste,
the smell, the lullabies, the myths, the legends that opened
Our childhood book of memories steeped in our own culture.

To hand over, ensconced in perfect harmony
We pass the memories richly bound, jaded not faded
Spreading neatly just as on the golden sands of time, the
White foamy waves recede back into the deep blue sea,
We return.

Sand Dunes

The scene flashes in my eye.

That sand buggy ride in Dubai, the desert in all its glory, fine sand in undulating waves, her screams of joy as the four by four tore into mother earth. Sand, the grit between our toes, warm, sunbaked seared by the white- hot horizon. Happiness of my wild first love, indescribable, teen fresh. She was my world. Her soft caresses, her words of comfort now a distant memory.

My strident march to serve my country, waving, to her as her eyes glistened with pride. Eighteen going on a lifetime. War ages you, lifting pieces of limbs of your mates. Yet the hope, that rising gush that a new life awaits, a future in a green peaceful land uplifts you.

The disinfectant lingers on my brain. Shocked and awed into submission, land-mined body, our future scrubbed into the orangey landscape.

Desert Dreams

Her body lay in the mortuary. Stateless, unclaimed.

Rumi had arrived in Dubai, from Kerala, to work on a
skyscraper.
Laid off, beholden to the moneylender and desperate
She fell off the unfinished thirty-eighth floor. Or was she
pushed?
Her dreams splattered on the sand.

She remained an untouchable, in birth and death.

Vikramaditya

The legendary king of yore
Twenty five tales of the Vampire
Penned in the *Pancha Vimshathi*
That the Sadhu asked him to bring back
The *vetala,* the demonic sprit that hangs
In the twilight zone between life and after life
Relishes and lays down its rules
'Solve my puzzles or go keep your peace'
Twenty four times it teases him
Flies back to hang in the cemetery tree
As he speaks to get the answer right
The ghostly precursor of Frankenstein?
The thirty two female statues that forces the king
Described in *Simhasana Dwathrishika*
To find humility in serving his people
All described in *Vedic* literature
Centuries old, passed down to generations
Handed down in song and tales
Of legends beyond the ken of our five senses
Of ghouls, demons, angels, airy beings
The reality of our marooned existence on planet
Earth blown away by other beings not material
Do we understand the laws of the universe?

Panchatantra

A collection of fables in prose and verse
The animal interrelated story, perhaps
Written in the third century before Christ
Like Russian dolls, stories within stories
Of five books on the wise conduct of life
Animal fables, like Disney of ancient times
Interweaved the world literature, a heritage
Prized and borrowed by future civilisations
From Persian to Arabic to Greeks and the West
Aesop's Fables, nursery rhymes and ballads
Literature and life enriched the world over.

Waiting

The search for a place in the car park
The waiting room, heaving with patients and family.
The crash of the ubiquitous vending machine
As the sickly sweet colas, and chocolates fall
To eager hands, the sugar breaks the boredom.
More anxiety rises like bile surging up, I try some
distraction. I listen to the weary small talk of the others.
Try to quiz the mobile, messages from well- wishers,
words to quell the anguish in the mind.
Pick up a glossy magazine with healthy, glowing
Photo-shopped celebrities, their blue-white smiles
mocking the grey –green patients with wan looks of pain.
The long corridor buzzes with nurses and auxiliaries holding
Folders with details of your body, the x-rays, the scans.
The body ravaged with age springing new dysfunctions.
Hoping to be healed and smoothed for the next few months,
Till the next visit.

Anamnesis

She built a temple of memories
Twisted like jagged leaves in the breeze
Floating freely like swirling, squawking birds.

Azure skies evoke all her senses
Broken dolls, a slate of scribbled alphabets
Beads, chains, pages of dog-eared books fluttered.

Scent of jasmine garlands, pomegranate seeds,
Colours enthralling but the grey returns
No beginning and no end.

Life

Our sentience just moves through our lives.
An unfinished house, door ajar, windows bare
Sun drenched veranda, weather beaten tiles
Bleached coral walls, sand and concrete piles
A contumacious garden, bees swarm like a lair
A house, not yet a home with hopes of perfection
Lying in wait, promising a new resurrection.

Opaque

The sound of sigh as snow falls on snow
Like a flower dying petal by petal,
The virgin white serape burying
The lush golden buds of spring.
A shimmer of crystals, dazzling in the faint glow
of a hesitant sun. Or is there an analemma
in the cosmos that the stratus clouds obscure?
A hallucinatory -dream walk in the opaque wilderness
The icicles crack underneath, an unknotted cincture
Submerged stories, within and without reveal the truth.
Grief spun in the cold aether, like mapmakers before us
Drawing lines on the ice, making and breaking
Memories of a song, snow beads, invoking *Ullr's* blessing,
The journey continues in the stillness, the hieroglyphed
language
Of winter, the unrequited love lingers into infinity.

Note:
Ullr is a Norse God of snow

A pastiche on Ogden Nash's 'Columbus'.

Darkest Hour?

Once upon a time there was an Englishman
And some people said he was a true gentleman
That he was a statesman and a war hero,
But other people thought he was just a zero.
He said Indians are a 'beastly people with a beastly religion.'
No, said his admirers you are dissing our leader a smidgen.
For the Bengal Famine of forty three, he refused any relief
He countered, for 'they breed like rabbits' that's my belief
'And if food is rare why is Gandhi not dead?'
Yes, these were the words this great hero really said.
So this truth of Churchill ought to be pointed out to every
child and every voter,
Because it has a very important moral, which is, he was 'Hitler
–like',*a fat bloater!

*:Leo Amery, a British man and Secretary of State for India at that
time, compared Hitler's biggest enemy (Churchill) to Hitler in this
context, at a sensitive time like the WW!*

Mango

Tiny green mango, picked on from on high,
Bit hard, sour, white saps burns the impatient tongue,
Evokes memories of childhood days, a sigh
Ensues, a new life oceans away, far flung.

The dark green skin envelops tight, a stone hearted core.
A knife splits open luscious, bright orange pulp, a sweet
Strong aroma spurts out and a million taste buds want more,
Enraptured, she is enslaved for life, this king of fruits, and a treat.

Now ripe in green grocer's boxed display
Glasgow's sun caressed fruits, stacked and rare
On plastic green grass of tropical fare,
An exotic array is in an aspiring bowl of clay.

Childhood dreams that oceans separated
Revived in one bite!

Refugee?

A blank page, a blank mind, the writer's block
A surfeit of experiences clogging the brain.
To trace them in ink feels an onerous task.
The paper is laid aside, an old box opened
the smell of some talc in a chiffon scarf triggers
an image of a girl in a new country, a silhouette,
of youth and innocence, laughter and happiness.

The pen spills the ink, paucity or plenitude?
The joy as the black shapes of words
imprint on the white page, images
floods from the heart to the fingertips.
Energised by the muse, a smile on the lips
Like music, tinkling the ivories, new sounds
and thoughts surging as the words flow,
Homeland! Is it a poem in the making?

River

A story can no more be submerged than a flowing river
Gold filigreed memories, shimmering in light
An annihilated dream, floods and desiccates
Torrents of fury, swirling thoughts stemmed
Silent now, like lotus-dappled pond at the edges.
Can the tale be forgotten?

Varanasi

The world's oldest continuously inhabited city, Mark Twain's
'Older than history, older than tradition and older than
legend'
Kashi, Benares, referenced in the Atharvaveda, the oldest
known text
Trading muslin, silks, perfumes, ivory and sculpture
The Buddha founded his faith here, Kabir wrote his poetry,
Tulsidas his incredible lyrics, the centre of learning and
knowledge
Founded on the confluences of the Ganges, of the two rivers
Varuna and Assi
The Himalayan ranges cold winds rams it on winter nights.

A city that has survived the destruction of temples by
Aurangzeb
The massacre of Indian soldiers by the British during the
Mutiny
The place where Sushruta practiced his medicine and surgery
in the 5th century BC
Manusmritihi the legal texts of the Dhamashastras was
written here
This ancient city in India is the microcosm of what is India,
Its survival, despite invasions, its pride and its contribution to
the world
Unparalleled yet modest in its very being, a place where souls
come to rest
And revere this place where Shiva's or Sati's earring fell on
this sacred earth.

War

The sea undulating, the orange flotillas against the blue
The interstices of waves and the still. She, seeking an anchoritic solitude
the soul inside her fecund belly heaving, the naval string tugging hard
 A new life in a land of milk and honey, if fate hands them the right card.

All she knew was language of the mountains, the sea
The sea, the sea, leading her to a tenebrous future, no fee
Settled in. Recalibrating all she knows, enervated in the new land
The baby's wriggling toes reassuring, no more struggle in the sand.

A glancing at her past, fleeing the tyrannies of Syrian wars
The glacial cold gripping her heart, in this new place of food and cars
A yearning, a meditation, the delicious feel of Arabic, in the incantation
Three pages of the Koran a pale simulacrum, a triptych, in her new nation.

Silence

And still it snows
Gently fall the snowflakes
Stars of crystalline perfection
Earth yielding to soft abundance
Enveloped in a cocooning white silence.

Baby Girl

The cry of a new born pierces shrill
Naked to the world, nine months borne full
The urge, the need to suckle, flesh to flesh
A miracle, five pounds, perfect, but unwanted.

The breadwinner stamps his will unchallenged
Another mouth to fee, another dowry to be found
Not hands to earn a crust, the burden of her nuptials
 In his eyes was too great a threat.

The Indian village looks askance as baby girl lies
Abandoned, her breath stopped
Before life can begin, buried deep in mother earth
The mother's screams are of no avail
Her womb, used, tired and emptied
Forced to try again for a much wanted boy.

Pancake

Pancake, pancake, pancake, turn, and toss,
Flying and landing on the floor, totally gross
Spread with lemon, runny honey or yummy Nutella
Homemade, cooking is fun for the fella.
Savoury, or sweet, fluffy, or dry as a bone,
Pile it up, toss a few, stuff your face and doggone.
Watch the sun streak the window and the signs of spring
Creeps up slow as the flowers blossom, and birds sing.

Letters

On rocks, palm leaves, leather, vellum, paper,
Epistles penned with a chisel, quill, pen,
The beauty of words to express feelings
All human experience forged in many ways.

Blue crinkles of the Basildon Bond airmail pages of a letter
Crossing the oceans, with words inscribed with love.
 The delectable thud as the postie drops the envelope
Heaving heart as one is transported to another world.

The rustle of a foolscap paper with blotches of ink spills
The fun of deciphering the scribbles on the lines
The joy of reading the good news and smiling inwardly
Or the tear drops making patterns of the hurt, a smudge.

No more scented letters, a pressed flower enclosed
A satin ribbon-tied bundle of emotions, kept
in secret boxes, locked and lie secure, untouched
for years and traces a life in another century.

The pretty stamps collection, the world in tiny thumbnails
Philately, a hobby that expanded one's horizons,
Stamps a thrill to own, on the Stanley Gibbons
 Albums, painstakingly and lovingly created.

Lost now, in the techno world of emails, Instagram, twitter
Switch a computer to get an invite or a sympathy card
The joy, 'Lost in post' forever now, a globalised world
Of instant moments, sated, forgotten in the ether.

Images

Hers were poems without borders, words mango-tipped
dripping on to a blue island, skies Saltire spread
With white contrails cross on blue, God encrypted?
Was her diverse voice, verses flowing penned for street cred?
She found that her poems appeared, on the bark of a tree,
words falling silently, like autumn leaves,
burnt sienna, red, ochre, gold, float free.
A string of words that made her heart heave.
Heart that gladdened at the rustle of a breeze,
the bend of a river, the soothing gurgle of a stream.
The fragrance of a floribunda white rose, a tease.
Words that traversed countries, vivid scenes, like a dream
She scribed her words, nature-hewn, her soul imbibing
a new culture, between and betwixt, holding sea shells at her ear.

Spice

The aroma arises, fulfilling the senses
The wok on the fire, the oil glaze
Seasoning splutters, mustard seeds
Cumin, pepper, asafoetida, mint
Cinnamon, turmeric, flavours and colour
As the onions and tomatoes soften.

The feel of home, she thinks, the strings
Of a veena, violin and flute, the music of
Krishna envelops the room. The babble
Of varied tongues, English mixed with Tamil,
Hindi, voices and words with familiar rhythms
Bubbles rising, in a subtropical succulent sauce.

Home in a cauldron, recipes handed down
Rehashed, adapted, a new fusion like the music
Krishna's sweet flute journeyed to Glasgow
 Group of seniors reminiscing their youth in
India, the passport of a new identity, worn with pride
As the heart still hankers after a spicy past.

Jumper

I searched for you in the warmth of wool
Hugged the smell of you in the blue yarn

Unpicked the knit and purl, simple design.
Threads that held you and me together

The white of the hospital room, the steel bed
Doctor's words were like crochet, lacy and ethereal.

Unravelled our world as if in slow motion
The yarn snapped the needles lay still.

Tresses

'Thick tresses that shame the black bee'
Says Bhartihari in the fifth century AD.
Locks that Shiva trapped the Ganga tight
letting out the seven rivers as gentle streams.

The lustrous mane of Sita exiled in the forest
the fourteen years had not stilled the beauty
Ravan compared her hair as thunderbolt.
The goddess with beauty within and without.

Black glossy hair plaited with care and love
the coconut oil gently massaged in, the soft
Sheen in the early morning dew tipped sunshine
Each strand tightly woven with legends of yore.

 A challenge to the plaits, fashion states.
 The curl is out, cut short, or straightened,
trichologists rule. Tresses a thing of the past,
adorning sculptures of ancient goddesses.

Ashwameda

I gallop on doing my duty, not the king's horse,
A poor wretched brown one, dark as the night
When the moon shimmers behind the clouds
I lay my head low, resting, sorrowful, the beatings
The lack of food, the poverty of my keeper
He works me to the bone, to scratch a living.
Then I espy with my big eye on that day
The prince's white horse is the chosen one
The ashvameda yaga needs a pure bred
White as the driven snow, sacrificed in the fire
I try to look away, but my eye is drawn to the fire.

Published in Visual Verse

Sunset

Diving for a living, as the world turns away
Swallowed by the deep, find the breath in the fish,
The strident blue, swimming across the ocean of life
Matsya avatar, a symbol of evolution, predating Darwin
The legend handed down from one generation to the next
Sacred to some and recorded in the Vedas for the world to imbibe
That knowledge of the ancients, streaking wild in our technological age
The blue of the seas, covering most of planet earth, the depths a mystery
Uncovered in stages, opening pages of wisdom from a mere aquatic being.

Published in Visual Verse

Words

Life is enriched by words in every which way, newspapers
From the tinkling of the bell on the newspaper boy's bike
Heralding the welcome newspaper that was read fully
To words on cereal packets and on billboards on journeys.

Mother's magazines were treasures to savour.
The postman handing in the colourful magazines,
Woman& Home, Woman's Weekly with recipes,
Patterns for frocks, short stories, comic strip for kids.

A book-filled world, shelves full of children's books
Fiction Non-fiction, magazines, Illustrated Weekly,
Opening the National Geographic, that smells of fresh
Print and colour photos from every corner of the world.

Words shining like millions of stars on a darkened sky
Little pieces of silver and gold in one's daily life
Trudging along the paths of strife and loneliness
Lexicon, vade mecum, opuscule that fulfil the soul.

Message

A crescent moon, a sliver of silver in the dark sky
The foaming waves build up high then subside
The beauty of the tide wading in and out of the shore
Faraway silhouette of a sailing boat etched like a painting
The cool sand between the toes, sandals slipped off
Holding the sarong tight against the lithe body
silver stars on deep purple twinkling above
moon dipped breeze sways the tall palm trees.
The milky white paper rustles, brushes against the glass
Sealed in tight, a blue ribbon holding the sweet message
A life penned in black ink on the virgin white paper
Describing the love and pain, the calligraphy a piece of art
Love-the highs and lows- the sweet and bitter, like the tide
a bottle holding a memoir bobs on the ocean waves.

Dust

Vedas mention fourteen worlds, sixty four dimensions
Three Lokas of earth, sky and heaven is our universe.
A tiny part of the vast universe we are but one of many.
The same dust and light has nurtured all living beings
Man believes himself to be superior to all, interdependence
Ignored, the resources overused, environment ruined.

Wasted lives indulging man's huge ego.
He struggles towards power and wealth
Lost in avarice for a few moments of glory.
Unaware of the Maya of life, transitory as a gossamer
Spider's web, we are but tiny specks in history.
Time devours all lives and returns us to dust.

Fragile

Today, love embraced me with open arms.
Warm, safe, adored held in a tight hug.
Today, the sun shone brighter, the flowers blossomed.
Love, precious but fragile as pages of a long-loved book.

Michelin Star

Recipes handed down, simple, never measured or written down.
I watched as she cooked, on firewood, then gas, in a bare kitchen.
Pots and pans that never matched, a handle loose or broken.
With no cupboards, rice and dhals in jute woven rough sacks.
Tasty, wholesome, healthy, and always served with love.
No glossy cookbook or Michelin Star chef can match that.

Things

Cotton, soft to the skin, the perfect bedlinen
Or starched heavy, flattened with coal-heated iron
Bleached, dyed in different shades, batik designed
Years of slave history running through its fine strands.

Sugar, cane rich, green and tall under the tropical sun,
Nurtured, tended and cultivated to sweeten our tongues
Crushed, the juice extracted, pure molasses, thick and brown
Like the bodies of those auctioned, welts marked like lines of cane.

Jute, the humble vegetable fibre, soft and shiny grown in East
Bengal
Made into coarse, hessian, gunny bags to hold rice and twisted into
rope.
A billion jute sandbags despatched from the British Empire in India
To the trenches in World War I, to protect soldiers in that futile war.

Bales of cotton streaked and branded with the blood of slaves
Bags of jute imprinted and inscribed with colonial stamps
Fields of cane sugar made into molasses and golden syrup
Things that have made the world sweeter, despite cost of human
lives.

Ice cream

The excitement of home-made ice cream
The old machine brought down, cleaned
Thoroughly, ice blocks specially ordered
Watching the thick milk condensed and cooled
The flavours added with fresh mangoes peeled
The golden flesh cut into tiny chunks, the juice
Added to the milk, sugar &cardamom to enhance
The delicious taste, the bright orange ice creamy
Liquid waiting to be thickened with several turns
of the handle. Each child thrilled to get a shot of
churning the milk in the steel can in the brown
wooden barrel. An hour of hard work delivers
the cold scoop of heavenly taste the slurps of
joy that remain forever in the memory.

.

Quill

The itch to write, mankind's attempts to communicate
On Palmyra leaves, preserved old languages for centuries
Hieroglyphic drawings on stone, blood, vegetable dyes
Vellum, skins of animals, etched with stone or crude metal
Quill inking paper, holy books writ with calligraphers' grace
Songs and poems transferred to paper, printed, published
As books, from huge tablet sixes to micro sized articles of beauty
Writing, finger poised on paper or computer to write.

Mute

The unsaid words hang on my throat

Lips bitten red raw, the bitterness

swallowed with rising bile, as the sea moaned

and waves crashed against the grey rocks

silvered by the crescent moon, hanging low

we sat in silence, lay on the cool sand.

Hours later we watched the horizon brighten,

Sky turned pale pink to gold streaking the blue

Gossamer clouds floated, transient as our rows

Drifted away, the pain inside subsided like

The white froth of the waves lashing on the

Rocks and gently returning to the blue sea.

Diaspora

One book closed, another opens, a new leaf each day
Nomadic, experiences new, strange, alien, enervating
New language, sounds, melodies, tastes to savour
Slowly settling to a new rhythm, adapting to change.

The memories flash in the inward eye, shadows never
Forgotten, picking an old book, thoughts like a flowing river
Invisible, shimmering in the starry nights, dream scenes
Waves beating like silent drums, turning the old pages
Dog-eared, much loved, scented, wrapped with emotion.

Then?

Liquid sounds tracing back to the beginning
Blue sea, creatures rising, brown earth below
Sounds become colours, white blossoming
Flowers transforming to an apple green, a snake
Slithering, tempting a bite, in the garden of sin.

Stones

Pebbles on the sea shore, smoothed over their roughness
by years of water flowing over them, a memento of a warm day.

A rose quartz ring, shades of pink, translucent, like the sky
At sunset, pinking down the horizon, as the pale moon rises.

Amethyst, a jewel to be created, the Royal purple resplendent
Set in polished silver, a bracelet to grace a fine wrist.

Stones with a million stories buried in its layers hard, cold
Flint, lava, fire inside, swirls with human tales of passion.

Humble stones, heaped over a hasty grave, a resting place
Rocks that rise up high, looking skywards, a spiritual high.

Stones, just stones.

Lost

Lost my country, I adopted a new one

Lost my mother tongue, words of another sweeten me,

Lost my culture, traditions. I enjoy & celebrate the other joyous festivals

Lost my parents, family so remote, friends fill the void, love surrounds me.

Cherry Blossom

Whole years wait for the buds to appear

Two weeks of ethereal beauty shades of pink and white

Wet petals rain down in the gentle breeze

A pastel pink carpet on the verdant green grass.

Acknowledgements

I must thank my poetry mentors Frances MacArthur, A.C.Clarke and Magi Gibson who helped me shape some of the poems. Palo Stickland, a fellow writer for her IT help and words of encouragement. Super support as always from Strathkelvin Writers, my first writing group and all the members of the Federation of Writers Scotland, thanks to all, it is very much appreciated. Thanks to all my friends and family who support me unstintingly.

Many of the poems have been published in various magazines and anthologies.
Light, published in Gutter magazine Issue (05).
The Missing Anklet, in 'The Bangalore Review.
Resolve, in 'The Poetry Shed' 2015.
Mother Earth, & Tartan &Turmeric in 'Steel Bellow' USA 2017.
The Kibble Palace, in West End: Pat's Guide.
Pearl, in Stanza- Poetry Map of Scotland.
Goodbye, in The Rat's Review.
Vermillion, in I am a Silent Poet.
Koorma Avatar, Ardhanarishvara, Ashwameda & Sunset, in Visual Verse.

Made in the USA
Columbia, SC
28 July 2018